Please visit our website, www.garethstevens.com. For a free color catalog of all our high-quality books, call toll free 1-800-542-2595 or fax 1-877-542-2596.

Cataloging-in-Publication Data

Names: Redshaw, Hermione, 1998-.
Title: Brazil / Hermione Redshaw.
Description: New York : Gareth Stevens Publishing, 2024. | Series: Travel the world!
Identifiers: ISBN 9781538288306 (pbk.) | ISBN 9781538288313 (library bound) | ISBN 9781538288320 (ebook)
Subjects: LCSH: Brazil--Juvenile literature. | Brazil--Description and travel--Juvenile literature.
Classification: LCC F2508.5 R437 2024 | DDC 981--dc23

Published in 2024 by
Gareth Stevens Publishing
2544 Clinton St.
Buffalo, NY 14224

Written by: Hermione Redshaw
Edited by: Elise Carraway
Designed by: Amy Li & Isabella Croker

Photo Credits

All images are courtesy of Shutterstock.com, unless otherwise specified. With thanks to Getty Images, Thinkstock Photo and iStockphoto. Recurring images – ONYXprj, Ihor Biliavskyi, alexmstudio. Cover images – Igoror, Sabelskaya, Lebedev Yury, Amanita Silvicora, Rachael Arnott, james weston. 2–3 – bissun. 4–5 – GoodStudio, Darth_Vector. 6–7 – Thoom, gillmar. 8–9 – Garsya, Luciano Mortula – LGM, oneinchpunch, Oscity, trabantos, Alfmaler. 10–11 – ilolab, Mapics, Shebeko, Sky and glass. 12–13 – Seahorse Vector, Sergey Dzyuba, Songquan Deng, Stoker-13, xamnesiacx84. 14–15 – ONYXprj, Dudaeva, Heracles Kritikos, Liubomir_P, Phant, SCStock. 16–17 – Dominik Matus (Wikimedia Commons), LEONARDO VITI, Moloko88, ovalagncy, Sirio Carnevalino. 18–19 – Arthur Balitskii, BAHDANOVICH ALENA, Boris Stroujko, Butter Bites, Darryl Brooks, Takashi Images. 20–21 – CoolR, DaLiu, Gabriele Maltinti, Jenny Sturm, Vadym Lavra, Vector_Up. 22–23 – GoodStudio, alkkdsg, Seahorse Vector.

© 2023 Booklife Publishing
This edition is published by arrangement with Booklife Publishing

All rights reserved. No part of this book may be reproduced in any form without permission in writing from the publisher, except by a reviewer.

Printed in the United States of America

CPSIA compliance information: Batch #CSGS24: For further information contact Gareth Stevens at 1-800-542-2595.

Find us on

CONTENTS

PAGE 4 — We Are Going on a Trip
PAGE 6 — Brasília
PAGE 8 — Salvador
PAGE 9 — Recife
PAGE 10 — Fortaleza
PAGE 11 — São Luís
PAGE 12 — The Amazon
PAGE 14 — Porto Velho
PAGE 15 — Cuiabá
PAGE 16 — Campo Grande
PAGE 17 — Porto Alegre
PAGE 18 — São Paulo
PAGE 20 — Rio de Janeiro
PAGE 22 — Writing Home
PAGE 24 — Glossary and Index

WORDS THAT LOOK LIKE THIS CAN BE FOUND IN THE GLOSSARY ON PAGE 24.

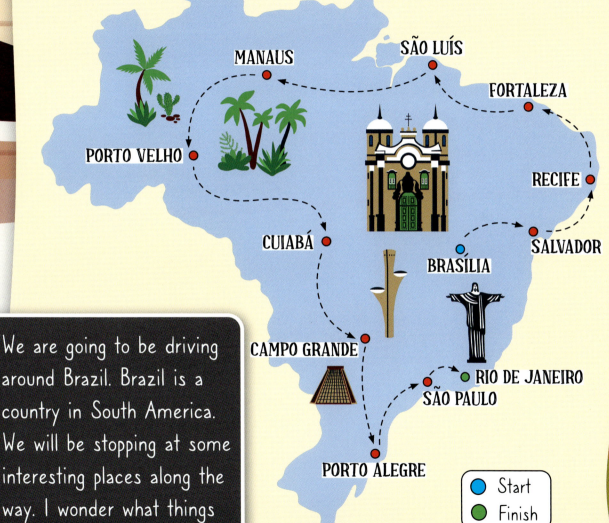

We are going to be driving around Brazil. Brazil is a country in South America. We will be stopping at some interesting places along the way. I wonder what things we will see!

BRASÍLIA

We start our road trip in Brasília. Apparently, Brasília used to be a <u>desert</u>. Now it is Brazil's capital city. It is hard to imagine that none of this was here 100 years ago.

Now entering: Brasília

CATHEDRAL OF BRASÍLIA

Brasília is full of interesting modern buildings. The Cathedral of Brasília is just one of them. There is also Paranoá Lake to see. Just like the rest of the city, the lake was made by humans.

PARANOÁ LAKE

SALVADOR

Our next stop is Salvador, which is a large city near the seaside. There are lots of colorful buildings in the Pelourinho neighborhood. I wish our house looked like this!

The Elevador Lacerda is a big elevator with great views!

RECIFE

The Boa Viagem Beach in Recife is huge! There are lots of tall buildings facing it with plenty of places to eat. We relax on the sand, swim in the sea, and eat some feijoada.

Feijoada is a black bean stew. It is very popular in Brazil!

Now entering: Ricife

FORTALEZA

Fortaleza has even more beaches, which are called praias in Brazil. However, Mom wanted to check out Cocó Park. Some <u>rare</u> plants and animals can be found here. We see monkeys and birds!

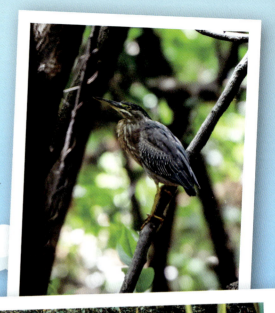

Now entering: Fortaleza

SÃO LUÍS

The Palácio dos Leões in São Luís used to be the <u>governor's</u> house. Some rooms are open to visitors. We get to see furniture and art from hundreds of years ago.

PALÁCIO DOS LEÕES

Now entering: São Luís

AMAZON

The Amazon is a big <u>rain forest</u> in South America. It has over a billion <u>acres</u> of forest. Most of it is in Brazil. Millions of different animals and plants live in the Amazon. Some can only be found here.

AMAZON RIVER DOLPHIN

CAPUCHIN MONKEY

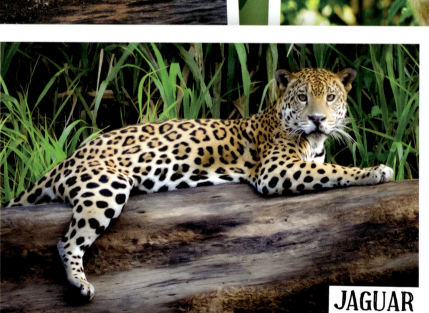

JAGUAR

It would be easy to get lost in the Amazon. It is also too big to know where to start! Manaus is a city in the center of the Brazilian Amazon. We find a guide there to help us in the forest.

AMAZON RIVER

PORTO VELHO

Porto Velho is on the way to lots of places. This is probably why <u>transportation</u> is important to its past. There are railway museums to see old trains. We visit one!

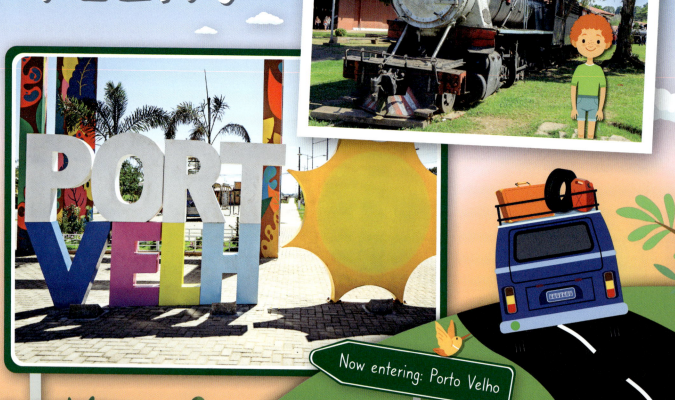

Now entering: Porto Velho

14

CUIABÁ

We visit Tia Nair Park in Cuiabá. We see so many capybaras here! The capybara is the world's largest rodent. There are lots of capybaras in South America, especially Brazil. They are very relaxed animals.

CAPYBARA IN TIA NAIR PARK

SO MANY CAPYBARAS!

CAMPO GRANDE

We see giant bird <u>statues</u> at the Plaza of the Macaws in Campo Grande! Then, we go to Campo Grande's Feira Central for food. Feira Central is a large food area with food from places such as Japan.

ME WITH THE BIRDS

FEIRA CENTRAL

Now entering: Campo Grande

PORTO ALEGRE

Some of the parks in Porto Alegre, such as Farroupilha Park, have lots going on. You can check out <u>stalls</u> selling things, visit fairs, or go on rides. We do all three!

FLEA MARKET AT FARROUPILHA PARK

PEDAL BOATS

SÃO PAULO

São Paulo is a busy city with lots of things to see and do. There is the São Paulo Cathedral and the Municipal Theatre. There are also modern buildings, such as those along Paulista Avenue.

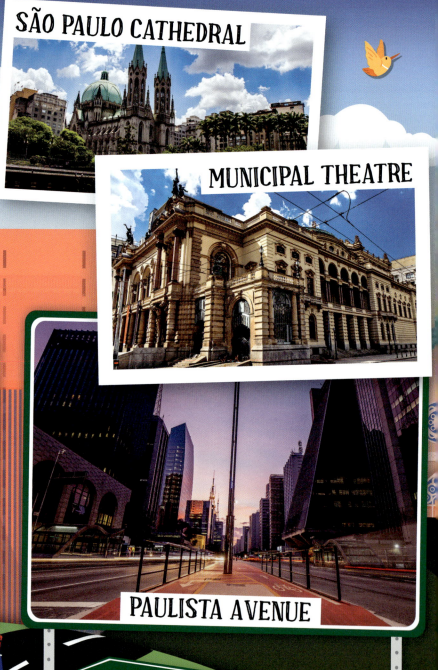

SÃO PAULO CATHEDRAL

MUNICIPAL THEATRE

PAULISTA AVENUE

Now entering: São Paulo

18

We're excited to see the Football Museum in São Paulo. Football—what we call soccer—is an important sport in Brazil. The museum tells the story of soccer in Brazil through the years. It is interesting!

RIO DE JANEIRO

Lots of people visit Rio de Janeiro to see the amazing things here, including one of the new <u>Seven Wonders of the World</u>! Christ the Redeemer is a big statue that looks over the city.

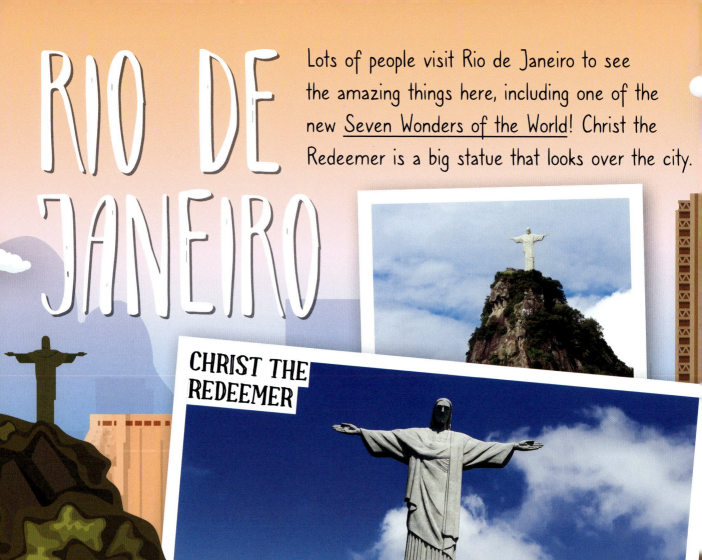

CHRIST THE REDEEMER

Now entering: Rio de Janeiro

We have a picnic in the forest of Tijuca National Park. There are some amazing views from the mountains! Later, we play soccer on Copacabana Beach, which is famous around the world.

TIJUCA NATIONAL PARK

COPACABANA BEACH

WRITING HOME

Brazil was great! From Brasília to Rio de Janeiro, our road trip was packed with lots of exciting things to do and see. We saw a world wonder, met some cute capybaras, and found plenty of beaches.

We did not get to see everything in Brazil. I wish we could have visited the Amazon Theatre in Manaus or seen the Carnaval. Hopefully, I can go back some day and explore more!

Love, Eddie.

GLOSSARY

ACRE	a measure of land area
DESERT	an area of land with very little rainfall and few plants
GOVERNOR	a person who is the leader of a state or town
MODERN	something that is new or fairly recently made
RAIN FOREST	a tropical forest that gets lots of rain and has very tall trees
RARE	not often found
RODENT	a usually small animal that has strong front teeth
SEVEN WONDERS OF THE WORLD	seven places built by people that are especially impressive
STALLS	small, open shops
STATUE	a figure, usually of a person or animal, that is made from things such as stone or metal
TRANSPORTATION	the act of moving people or things from one place to another

INDEX

Amazon, the 12–13, 22
animals 10, 12, 15
art 11
beaches 9–10, 21–22
birds 10, 16
capybaras 15, 22

Christ the Redeemer 20
forests 12–13, 21
museums 14, 19
parks 10, 15, 17, 21
plants 10, 12
trains 14